Sacrament Talk Mastery

How to Give

a Sacrament Talk

When You Really Don't Want to

By

Michael D. Callaghan

SACRAMENT TALK MASTERY: HOW TO GIVE A SACRAMENT TALK WHEN YOU REALLY DON'T WANT TO

First edition. January 25, 2024.

Copyright © 2024 Michael D Callaghan.

ISBN: 979-8224789894

Written by Michael D Callaghan.

Also by Michael D Callaghan

Angular Advocate
Developing Progressive Web Applications with Angular: How to Build and Deploy Mobile Applications without Paying Apple or Google for the Privilege

P-AI-R Programming
P-AI-R Programming: How AI Tools Like GitHub Copilot and ChatGPT Can Radically Transform Your Development Workflow
Pair Programming with Chat GPT

Standalone
Don't Say That at Work
Customizing ChatGPT: Quickly and Easily Create and Share Custom Business-Specific GPTs Without Code
How to Deploy Any Web Application to the Apple App Store: Make Your Application Available to Millions of iOS Users in About an Hour with Ionic's Capacitor
Sacrament Talk Mastery: How to Give a Sacrament Talk When You Really Don't Want To
Techno Tales

The Scout Law of Leadership: 12 Attributes Every Leader (or Aspiring Leader) Should Cultivate

¡NO DIGAS ESO EN EL TRABAJO! LECCIONES QUE PUEDES USAR PARA MEJORAR TUS HABILIDADES DE COMUNICACIÓN EN LOS NEGOCIOS

Watch for more at https://walkingriver.com.

Table of Contents

Is This Book for You?

Thank you for checking out this book. In case you have questions, feel free to contact me on Twitter @WalkingRiver[1], or you can email me anytime at michael@walkingriver.com. I try to respond quickly to everyone who reaches out.

As members of the Church of Jesus Christ of Latter-day Saints, sacrament meeting talks are an integral part of our worship experience. Yet, many of us have endured talks that fell flat, missed the mark, or simply failed to engage the audience.

Before we begin, let's spend a moment to decide whether this book is right for you. Do any of these sound like you?

- The bishop just asked you to speak at church and gave you very little time to prepare.
- You get nervous about giving a public speech or presentation.
- You wonder whether anyone will want to hear what you have to say.
- You sometimes get tongue-tied and don't know what to say.
- You don't really know where to start when planning a talk.
- Despite the above, you want to succeed.

This is a short, straightforward book with useful and actionable tips you can employ right away.

The techniques and suggestions come from my own personal and professional experience over three decades as a software developer and trainer.

---

1. https://twitter.com/walkingriver

I've made every mistake I warn about in the book. By including them, it is my hope that you can learn from my mistakes.

In this book, we will explore what makes a sacrament meeting talk effective, and what common pitfalls to avoid. Through examples of both good and bad talks, we will discover practical tips and strategies for crafting a message that connects with the congregation and inspires them to action.

So, whether you are a seasoned speaker or a first-time talk giver, this book will provide you with the tools you need to deliver a message that uplifts and edifies.

If that sounds good to you, then read on!

So You've Been Asked to Speak

The bishop just asked you to talk in church. Now what? Whether this is your first time as a youth, or whether you've been speaking for decades, you may experience a range of emotions. I'll touch on some of them briefly here, then offer advice to help you overcome them throughout the rest of the book.

Anxiety

It is common to feel anxious or nervous about speaking in front of a congregation, especially if public speaking is outside of one's comfort zone. The fear of being judged or making mistakes can contribute to this anxiety.

Anxiety may stem from the fear of public speaking, a common phobia for many individuals. The pressure of speaking in front of a congregation and the potential judgment or scrutiny can trigger feelings of anxiety. Past negative experiences or a lack of confidence in your speaking abilities can also contribute to this emotion.

To address anxiety, it can be helpful to prepare thoroughly. Practice your talk multiple times, both alone and in front of trusted friends or family members. Deep breathing exercises and positive self-talk can also help manage anxiety. Remember that the congregation is supportive and wants you to succeed. Trust in your preparation and rely on the Spirit to guide you.

Pressure

The responsibility of delivering a meaningful talk in a sacred setting can also create a sense of pressure. The desire to make a positive impact and provide spiritual nourishment to the congregation can weigh heavily on you, leading to feelings of pressure to deliver a talk that meets those expectations.

To manage pressure, set realistic expectations for yourself. Understand that perfection is not the goal, but rather delivering a heartfelt message. Break down the preparation process into manageable steps and prioritize the most essential aspects. Seek guidance from the Spirit and remember that your talk is part of a collective worship experience, not a sole measure of your worth.

Insecurity

Some people may feel unsure of their ability to effectively convey their message or engage the audience. You may question your knowledge or worry about being inadequate compared to other speakers.

Insecurity can arise from self-doubt and a perceived lack of expertise on the assigned topic. Comparing yourself to other speakers who may be more experienced or knowledgeable can lead to feelings of inadequacy. Concerns about not meeting the expectations of the congregation or the leaders who assigned the talk can also fuel insecurity.

Combat feelings of insecurity by focusing on your unique perspective and experiences. Remember that the assignment was given to you for a reason, and your personal insights are valuable. Seek support from others who can provide encouragement and remind you of your strengths. Embrace a growth mindset, recognizing that every opportunity to speak is a chance for personal growth.

It is important to recognize that these emotions are normal and experienced by many who are asked to speak in sacrament meeting. By acknowledging and addressing these emotions, you can navigate your speaking assignments with greater confidence and reliance on the Lord's guidance.

Excitement

Alongside the nerves, there may be a sense of excitement or anticipation about the opportunity to share personal insights and thoughts on a particular topic.

Excitement often arises from the opportunity to share personal insights, thoughts, and testimony with others. It can stem from a genuine enthusiasm to contribute to the worship service, inspire fellow members, and deepen personal understanding and connection to the topic.

Gratitude

Cultivate gratitude by focusing on the privilege of being entrusted with the opportunity to speak. Reflect on the blessings and personal growth that come from the experience. Express gratitude in prayers for guidance and inspiration. Gratitude can help shift your mindset from apprehension to a positive and humble outlook.

Faith and Trust

Strengthen your faith and trust in the Lord through prayer and scripture study. Seek guidance from the Spirit in your preparation and delivery. Lean on the promises of divine assistance and trust that the Lord will magnify your efforts. Remind yourself that you are an instrument in His hands, and He will guide your words.

The Many Facets of Sacrament Talks

In the church's *General Handbook,* you will see this brief overview of sacrament meeting talks:

> *The bishopric selects speakers for sacrament meeting. Most often they invite ward members, including youth...*
>
> *The bishopric extends invitations to speak well in advance of the meeting. Speakers bear testimony of Jesus Christ and teach His gospel using the scriptures. Messages should build faith and be consistent with the sacred nature of the sacrament.*
>
> *https://www.churchofjesuschrist.org/study/manual/general-handbook/29-meetings-in-the-church?lang=eng&id=p32-p33#p32*

That isn't much to go on, so we'll start with what types of talks you might be expected to give.

Sacrament meetings provide diverse opportunities for members to share their insights, testimonies, and experiences. In this chapter, we will explore the three primary types of sacrament talks you may be asked to deliver. By understanding the unique characteristics and objectives of each talk type, you can tailor your message to create a more engaging, meaningful, and memorable experience for your audience.

Informational

Educational or informational talks aim to teach the audience about a specific topic or concept, providing them with valuable knowledge that they can apply in their own lives. In a sacrament meeting, this might involve discussing church doctrine, sharing insights from scriptures, or delving into the lives of important religious figures. When preparing an educational talk, focus on presenting clear, concise information and consider incorporating visual aids, anecdotes, or personal experiences to help your audience better understand and remember the material.

Example

Elder Quentin L. Cook's talk from the October 2018 General Conference, titled "Deep and Lasting Conversion to Heavenly Father and the Lord Jesus Christ," is an excellent example of an informational talk. In this talk, he introduces and explains the new meeting schedule for Sunday worship services.

In that talk, he discusses the new meeting schedule:

> *The Sunday Church meetings will consist of a 60-minute sacrament meeting each Sunday, focused on the Savior, the ordinance of the sacrament, and spiritual messages. After time for transition to classes, Church members will attend a 50-minute class that will alternate each Sunday:*

This quote provides a clear and concise explanation of the changes to the Sunday meeting schedule, which is essential information for members of the Church. If you are giving an informational talk, you can use this talk as a guide.

Inspirational

Inspirational talks are the most common type of talk given during sacrament meetings. Rather than asking listeners to do something for you, you are sharing information for their benefit, possibly inspiring them to make changes in their lives. Your role is to provide them with valuable insights and encouragement to make positive changes for themselves. To emphasize this, use the word "you" more often than "I" in your speech. Refrain from using the phrase "in my opinion," as it may imply that you are attempting to persuade your audience.

Example

An excellent example of an inspirational talk from *General Conference is President Thomas S. Monson's talk from April 2008, titled "Finding Joy in the Journey."* In this talk, he encourages members to find joy in their lives and to focus on the positive aspects of life rather than dwelling on the negative.

> *Let us relish life as we live it, find joy in the journey, and share our love with friends and family. One day, each of us will run out of tomorrows.*

This quote is a powerful reminder to focus on what truly matters in life and to cherish the relationships we have with our loved ones.

Entertaining

While the primary goal of an entertaining talk is to amuse the audience, it is important to consider the context in which you are speaking. Strive to be engaging but recognize that attempting to entertain may not always be appropriate, depending on the setting. A majority of talks can incorporate some level of entertainment, and most presentations should be engaging in one way or another. This does not mean every talk must be humorous; often, serious talks can be just as powerful. However, adding a touch of humor or other forms of entertainment can make even the most serious talks more engaging.

In an October 2008 General Conference talked titled "Come What May, and Love It," Elder Joseph B. Wirthlin related an amusing story about one of his daughter's blind dates:

She was all dressed up and waiting for her date to arrive when the doorbell rang. In walked a man who seemed a little old, but she tried to be polite... We watched as she got into the car, but the car didn't move. Eventually our daughter got out of the car and, red faced, ran back into the house. The man that she thought was her blind date had actually come to pick up another of our daughters who had agreed to be a babysitter for him and his wife.

This light-hearted story demonstrates how humor can be used to make a talk more engaging and entertaining, even when discussing serious matters.

Testimony

Sharing your personal testimony allows you to express your faith in the principles, doctrines, or experiences you are discussing. A sincere testimony demonstrates your conviction and can inspire others to reflect on their own beliefs and experiences. As you share your testimony, focus on the core aspects of your faith, such as your belief in Jesus Christ, the restored gospel, or the power of prayer. You can also share specific experiences where you felt God's guidance or witnessed His hand in your life. Remember to speak from the heart, as genuine emotions can create a lasting impact on your audience.

Elder Jeffrey R. Holland, in his October 2013 General Conference talk titled "Like a Broken Vessel," shares a powerful and personal testimony of the Church and the Savior. Here's a quote from that talk:

I testify of the holy Resurrection, that unspeakable cornerstone gift in the Atonement of the Lord Jesus Christ! With the Apostle Paul, I testify that that which was sown in corruption will one day be raised in incorruption and that which was sown in weakness will ultimately be raised in power. I bear witness of that day when loved ones whom we knew to have disabilities in mortality will stand before us glorified and grand, breathtakingly perfect in body and mind. What a thrilling moment that will be!

In this quote, Elder Holland bears witness to the Atonement and Resurrection of Jesus Christ and the promise of perfect healing that it offers to all who suffer from disabilities and challenges in this life. You don't need to try to emulate Elder Holland in your own testimony, but as you can see, including one in your talk can be extremely powerful.

The Worst Talk Ever

Throughout the book, we will analyze the various mistakes made in this talk and provide guidance on how to avoid them.

In this chapter, I will provide you an example of what not to do when giving a sacrament meeting talk. While this talk on faith may elicit a chuckle or two, it fails to connect with the congregation and deliver a meaningful message.

So, without further ado, let us examine what may just be the worst sacrament meeting talk ever delivered.

My Talk on Faith

Good morning, brothers and sisters. [If no one responds, repeat it until you get a response.]

For those of you who don't know me, my name is ________________________ and have been in this ward for the past year. Today I intend for my talk to be like a ghostly elevator—-—it will lift your spirits! [Chuckle at your own horrible joke]

The bishop asked me to speak for five minutes on faith. I don't know why the Bishop thought I was the right person to speak on faith. I spent most of the week trying to get out of it, but I didn't do a very good job, so here I am.

I hate giving talks so I put this off till this afternoon, so hopefully the Spirit will be here to teach you something and I apologize for this talk's poor quality. I was too bogged down with my video games and band to even consider doing this.

Even so, I am grateful for the opportunity for me to get up to speak to you today. Talks are supposed to be a great opportunity for y'all to learn from me, but I definitely learned more writing this talk.

According to Google, the definition of faith is "complete trust or confidence in someone or something", which is far more accurate than the definition of faith as given by Abbott's Webster Selected Dictionary circa 1923 which says that faith is "complete coincidence."

To demonstrate my tremendous faith, I'd like to say a few words about the Great Pumpkin. Halloween will soon be with us, and on Halloween night, the Great Pumpkin rises out of the pumpkin patch, and brings toys to all the good little children. I have complete confidence, or faith, that, on Halloween night, the Great Pumpkin will be there. You'll see. You'll all see. I'll be there ready to meet him when he comes. None of you have the faith that I do in the Great Pumpkin.

If y'all turn to 2 Chronicles 12:3-7—go ahead, I'll wait. ... ... Are we all there? (Repeat if no response) Yes? Good. Going on. In 2 Chronicles 12:3-7, it reads "With twelve hundred chariots, and threescore thousand horsemen: and the people were without number that came with him out of Egypt; the Lubims, the Sukkiims, and the Ethiopians. And he took the fenced cities which pertained to Judah, and came to Jerusalem.

Then came Shemaiah the prophet to Rehoboam, and to the princes of Judah, that were gathered together to Jerusalem because of Shishak, and said unto them, Thus saith the Lord, Ye have forsaken me, and therefore have I also left you in the hand of Shishak. Whereupon the princes of Israel and the king humbled themselves; and they said, The Lord is righteous." Think about that next time you lack faith.

I would like to share with you a story I heard during some session of general conference recently from a General Authority and then again several times in sacrament meeting over the past few months. Most of you are familiar with Alice in Lewis Carroll's classic novel Alice's Adventures in Wonderland. You will remember that she comes to a crossroads with two paths before her, each stretching onward but in opposite directions. As she contemplates which way to turn, she is confronted by the Cheshire Cat, of whom Alice asks, "Which path shall I follow?" The cat answers, "That depends where you want to go. If you do not know where you want to go, it doesn't matter which path you take." That, my friends, takes real faith.

In conclusion, I'd like to bear my testimony that I know this church is true. In the name of thy son, Jesus Christ. Amen.

Not a Real Talk

I hope you experienced a few cringe-worthy moments while reading that. To be clear, this talk was never actually delivered in Sacrament Meeting. It was specifically written to be bad.

Later in this book, I will explain why this was such a horrible talk, beyond its obvious problems, and provide you with a series of tips that will help make your next talk great – even if you don't want to give it!

Preparing Content for a Sacrament Meeting Talk

If you've ever stood in front of a congregation and shared your thoughts, insights, and testimony, you know it can be nerve-wracking. You want to ensure that your listeners are engaged, inspired, and spiritually nourished by your words. When it comes to delivering a sacrament meeting talk, there are many things to consider, such as what your audience expects, how to structure your content, and how to pace yourself. If you're ready to become a more effective speaker in sacrament meetings, read on.

What should you talk about? When asked to give a sacrament meeting talk, you are usually given a topic or theme. From there, you may have various directions to explore. This is where it becomes enjoyable and creative. You can decide to give the talk in a more traditional format, or you might want to share personal experiences and stories that relate to the topic. You could also incorporate testimonies or insights from church leaders and scriptures.

Brainstorming: How to make your talk unique

The first step in brainstorming is to allow yourself time to be creative. Think about what you want your talk to convey before deciding how to achieve that. Some ideas may seem unconventional or even impossible, but don't dismiss them too quickly. Often, the most unexpected ideas are the best ones. Keep brainstorming and avoid getting hung up on just one idea.

Here are some questions to help you think of creative ways to make your talk unique and engaging:

- What is something unusual or surprising about this topic from a gospel perspective?

- What have other church leaders or members said about this topic? How could I do something different from what they did?
- How could I help my audience feel the Spirit more strongly regarding this topic?
- How could I make my audience laugh or cry when they hear me speak?
- How could I make my audience feel like they are part of the experience with me?
- If I had no limits whatsoever, how would I put this talk together?

Once you have some ideas, select a couple and see where they take you.

Organizing your thoughts

A typical sacrament meeting talk usually begins with an introduction and ends with a conclusion and a testimony. The introduction provides an overview of the talk and sets the tone. It's essential that this section is brief, interesting, and relevant, so listeners are drawn in right away. The conclusion should summarize what was covered and leave people feeling spiritually nourished. You should always end your talk with a testimony of the church, the savior, your topic, etc.

The body of your talk generally consists of three main parts: an opening statement or story, an explanation or description, and a summary or lesson learned. An opening statement grabs attention immediately and sets up the topic for discussion. The explanation or description section delves into the details, providing more background about your topic. The summary or lesson learned portion sums up everything covered and gives people an idea of how they can apply what they've learned in their lives.

The conclusion wraps up everything discussed and is an opportunity to bear your testimony and leave the audience with something to ponder. Remember that there may be times when you need to pause for a moment of reflection or ask rhetorical questions of your audience. You may also want to include a story, quote, or scripture at some point in your presentation. Use these elements as needed, but don't overdo it and make your talk too long. Instead, keep it focused by sticking with the main parts and using any other parts sparingly and when appropriate.

Visual Aids

As a general rule, visual aids and props are not used in sacrament meetings. Sacrament meeting talks are focused on the spoken word and personal testimonies, allowing the Spirit to touch the hearts of the listeners. Save visual aids for other settings, such as Sunday School lessons or firesides, where they might be more appropriate and engaging.

If you feel strongly about using a visual aid or prop in your sacrament meeting talk, consult with your bishop or other church leaders to ensure your presentation aligns with the expectations for sacrament meeting. Remember, the focus should always be on the gospel, sharing personal experiences, and bearing your testimony to create a spiritually uplifting experience.

By keeping these guidelines in mind, you will be better prepared to deliver an inspiring and engaging sacrament meeting talk without the need for visual aids or props, allowing the Spirit to be the center of attention.

Summary

Preparing content for a sacrament meeting talk involves prayerful consideration, brainstorming, and organizing your thoughts. Keep your focus on the gospel, share personal experiences, and bear your testimony to connect with your audience and create a spiritually uplifting experience. By following these guidelines and relying on the Spirit, you will be well on your way to delivering an inspiring and engaging sacrament meeting talk.

What Should You Talk About?

When you're asked to give a sacrament meeting talk, it's natural to feel nervous or unsure of where to begin. You want to make sure that your talk is not only engaging and inspiring but that it's also spiritually nourishing for your audience. However, by incorporating some essential elements into your talk, you can create an impactful and memorable message.

It is essential to begin your preparation by seeking guidance through prayer. This will help you connect with the Spirit and gain a deeper understanding of the topic you've been assigned. Relying on the Spirit will also help you to discern what aspects of the topic to focus on and how to effectively communicate your message.

Focus on Gospel Principles

The most important element of a sacrament meeting talk is to focus on gospel principles and how they apply to our daily lives. Take time to deeply consider the topic you've been assigned and think about how you can draw connections to the gospel and the teachings of the Church. This will help you create a talk that is both relevant and impactful for your audience.

Use the Hymn Book

Hymns are a powerful resource to draw upon when preparing a sacrament meeting talk. Hymns are filled with uplifting messages that can help illustrate and reinforce the gospel principles you wish to convey. By incorporating hymns into your talk, you can engage your audience in a meaningful way and create a deeper connection between them and the message you're sharing. You can also use hymns as a tool to inspire reflection and contemplation, allowing your listeners to internalize the message and connect with it on a personal level. Whether you use hymns to open or close your talk or to illustrate specific points throughout, they can be a valuable resource for enhancing your message and creating a more spiritually uplifting experience for your audience.

Generous Use of Scriptures

Using scriptures in your sacrament meeting talk can be a powerful way to add depth and relevance to your message. Take time to carefully choose appropriate scriptures that relate to your topic, and think about how you can use them effectively to convey your message. This will help create a talk that is both engaging and spiritually uplifting.

Material from Church Magazines

Another valuable resource to draw upon when preparing a sacrament meeting talk is the church magazines. The *Liahona, Friend,* and other church publications are filled with inspiring stories, teachings, and insights from church leaders and members. By utilizing these materials, you can enhance your talk with relevant and timely examples that will engage your audience and help illustrate your message. You can also use these publications to provide additional context or background information about the topic you've been assigned to speak on. Additionally, incorporating teachings and insights from the church magazines can help reinforce the idea that you're part of a larger community of members who are all striving to live the gospel and serve one another.

General Conference and Devotionals

General Conference talks, devotionals, and fireside broadcasts can also be valuable resources to draw upon when preparing a sacrament meeting talk. These talks and broadcasts are typically given by church leaders and scholars and are filled with insights and teachings that can help provide additional depth and understanding to your topic. By incorporating specific quotes or teachings from these resources, you can enhance your talk with authoritative and relevant perspectives that will engage your audience and help illustrate your message. Additionally, drawing from these resources can help create a sense of continuity and connection with the larger church community, as you demonstrate that you're drawing upon the same sources of inspiration and guidance as other church members around the world.

Personal Stories and Testimonies

Another key element of a successful sacrament meeting talk is to include personal stories and testimonies that connect with your audience. Think about your own experiences and how they relate to the topic you've been assigned. This will help you create a talk that is both relatable and inspiring for your listeners.

Avoid Controversial Topics

While it can be tempting to use your sacrament talk as a platform to express your opinions on controversial topics, this is generally not appropriate for sacrament meeting. It's important to avoid political or divisive issues and to focus instead on sharing personal experiences and gospel principles that will help uplift and inspire your audience.

Using a sacrament talk as a platform to express your opinions on controversial topics can be a divisive and uncomfortable experience for the congregation. Members of the audience may feel offended or uncomfortable, and the overall spirit of the meeting may be disrupted. The purpose of sacrament meeting is to come together as a ward to worship and edify one another, and promoting personal opinions or divisive issues can detract from this purpose. Additionally, it may damage your credibility and your ability to effectively communicate gospel principles in the future. Therefore, it's essential to approach the opportunity to speak in sacrament meeting with prayerful consideration and to focus on sharing personal experiences and gospel principles in a way that will uplift and inspire those in attendance.

Keep It Simple and Clear

In order to effectively communicate your message to your audience, it's important to keep your talk simple and clear. Avoid using overly complicated language or concepts and focus on communicating your ideas in a way that is easy to understand. This will help ensure that your message resonates with your audience and that they leave feeling spiritually nourished.

Pop-Culture References

While it may not be intuitive, pop-culture references can be used effectively in sacrament meeting talks when they fit the narrative. When used appropriately, pop-culture references can help engage your audience and make your message more relatable.

Pres. Thomas S. Monson referred to the play Shenandoah often in his talks at General Conference, and once also mentioned *My Fair Lady* in the same talk (April 1994).

In April 2010, President Dieter F. Uchtdorf delivered an entire General Conference talk revolving around fairy tales.

I've personally witnessed sacrament talks that mentioned Harry Potter, Star Wars, Star Trek, Shrek, and more Disney movies than I can remember.

In one of my own talks, I used Arthur Dent's attempts to fly from *Hitchhiker's Guide to the Galaxy*. It was very well received. My family members find a way to weave a Disney movie into almost every talk they give. Don't be afraid to use stories that you find inspiring or helpful in making your point.

It's important to note that these references were used judiciously and with purpose, to help illustrate a gospel principle or make a point in a relatable and memorable way.

If you can make your references match your message, use them. However, it's important to use them sparingly and only when they add value to your message.

By including these elements in your sacrament meeting talk, you'll be well on your way to delivering an inspiring and engaging talk that will uplift and inspire your audience. With these guidelines in mind, and with prayerful consideration and reliance on the Spirit, you'll be well-prepared to give a successful sacrament meeting talk.

Recipes for an Effective Talk

Crafting a sacrament talk that is engaging, meaningful, and spiritually uplifting can be a daunting task. Whether you are an experienced speaker or a first-time talk giver, finding the right words to convey your message can be a challenge. Fortunately, there are a few tried-and-true methods that can help you get started and stay on track. The following recipes are designed to provide you with inspiration and guidance as you prepare your talk. Keep in mind that these are only suggestions, and you should feel free to adapt and modify them as needed to suit your individual style and circumstances. Above all, remember to seek the guidance of the Holy Spirit and to approach your talk with humility and faith.

Start with an Assigned Topic

If you have been given a general topic instead of a specific conference talk, don't worry. You can still craft an effective sacrament talk by using the resources available to you. Start by researching the topic in the scriptures, looking up related hymns and General Conference talks. Once you have gathered this material, think about personal experiences or stories that relate to the topic. Finally, tie it all together with a clear message that reflects your personal insights and testimony. By following this process, you can deliver a meaningful talk that inspires and uplifts your audience.

1. Begin by looking up your topic in the hymn book.

1. Read the related hymns and choose one that resonates with you.
2. Note the scripture references at the bottom of the hymn, read them, and incorporate them into your talk.
3. Cross-reference those scripture passages with general

conference talks to find relevant insights.

4. Share a personal story or experience, or retell a story from a conference talk, to illustrate your message.
5. Connect all the elements, weaving together hymns, scriptures, and stories in a cohesive manner.
6. Express your feelings about what you've learned during your preparation.
7. If needed, repeat the steps to expand your talk to the assigned length.
8. Conclude by bearing your testimony about the topic and the Church, and close in the name of Jesus Christ.

By following this recipe, you can create an engaging, meaningful, and well-structured talk that will inspire and uplift your audience. We'll see an example later. Keep in mind, this is only one possible recipe. As you gain experience, I'm sure you will find your own. Inject your own personality and your own favorite sources. Have fun with it.

Start with a General Conference Talk

When you are asked to speak, the person assigning the talk may also provide you with a General Conference talk to use as the basis of your remarks. If this is the case, you can use the following steps to prepare your talk. By following this recipe, you will be able to craft a talk that is both meaningful and relevant to your audience, and that draws upon the wisdom and inspiration shared in the General Conference talk.

1. Read and study the assigned General Conference talk thoroughly to fully understand the topic and message.
2. Look up the scripture references mentioned in the talk and study them in context to gain a deeper understanding of the principles being discussed.
3. Use the scripture references to find additional related scriptures

that support or enhance the talk's message.

4. Look up the hymns mentioned in the talk and read the lyrics. Consider using one or more of the hymns in your talk as a way to reinforce the message.

5. Conclude the talk by reiterating the main points and expressing gratitude for the opportunity to share the message.

Start with a Scripture

If you've been given a specific scripture to speak on in your sacrament talk, you may feel a bit overwhelmed at first. How do you take a single verse or passage and turn it into a full talk? Fortunately, there are steps you can follow to help you prepare and deliver a powerful message.

This recipe will guide you through the process of expanding on a single scripture, drawing on additional scriptures, talks, and stories to help illustrate your point. Remember to pray for guidance as you prepare, and let the scriptures and the Spirit guide your words.

1. Read the scripture slowly and thoughtfully, taking note of any phrases or ideas that stand out to you.

1. Look up the scripture in the Topical Guide or the Bible Dictionary and read the cross-references.

2. Search for that scripture in General Conference.

3. Look up hymns that reference that scripture.

4. Make a list of your favorites from the previous two steps.

5. Now consider following one of those recipes.

Remember, the goal is to use the provided scripture as a launching point for exploring deeper themes and insights, while always staying true to the spirit and message of the original text.

Should You Script Your Sacrament Meeting Talk?

Preparing an entire sacrament meeting talk can be time-consuming and challenging, especially if you're not used to scripting a speech. Deciding whether or not to script your entire talk depends on your personal preferences and speaking style. Here are some points to consider when making your decision:

Benefits of Scripting

Organizing your thoughts: Scripting your talk from start to finish helps you organize your thoughts and ideas and provides a clear outline for your presentation, ensuring you don't go off on tangents or forget important points.

Confidence: Having an entire speech written out can help you feel more confident while speaking, as you'll have a clear outline to follow and can use the script as a reference if needed.

Polished delivery: Scripting your entire talk can lead to a more polished and well-organized speech, helping you stand out and create a memorable spiritual experience for the congregation.

Avoiding forgotten points: Scripting helps ensure that you cover all important points and don't overlook anything crucial.

When to Script Your Talk

Generally, you may consider scripting your sacrament meeting talk if you're speaking on a more complex topic, if you're inexperienced in public speaking, or if you tend to get nervous during your talks.

Benefits of Not Scripting

Natural delivery: Not scripting your entire talk allows for a more natural and conversational delivery, which may be better received by your audience.

Flexibility: Not scripting gives you the ability to adapt to the congregation's reactions and make adjustments as needed.

Trust and connection: Focusing on building trust with the congregation and practicing different approaches beforehand can help create a more engaging and relatable experience.

Instead of scripting your entire talk, you could create a detailed outline of your main points and stories. This approach provides a balance between structure and flexibility, allowing you to deliver a heartfelt and engaging sacrament meeting talk.

In conclusion, deciding whether or not to script your sacrament meeting talk ultimately depends on your personal preferences and speaking style. Consider the benefits of both approaches and choose the one that best aligns with your goals and the spiritual message you wish to convey.

Real World Example in Sacrament Meetings

I was once asked to share a few thoughts about the upcoming Christmas season during a sacrament meeting. With only twenty minutes to prepare and knowing I had a supportive audience, I jotted down a few bullet points:

- Mention Christmas and what it means to me – focus on giving and serving others.
- Share a personal story about delivering a piano on Christmas Eve.

- Emphasize that not all acts of service need to be grand gestures.
- Conclude by expressing my love for Christmas and how I look forward to it every year.

This was enough to provide about ten minutes of content. To break it down, I first introduced my topic by talking about Christmas and how it's my favorite holiday because it puts me in the mood for giving. In just two or three sentences, I set the stage for my talk. Next, I shared a personal story about a friend who helped me deliver a piano I had bought for my wife for Christmas. He had kept it in his basement for a month, and we sneaked it into the house around midnight. This anecdote illustrated the importance of service and friendship.

After that, I highlighted that giving gifts or providing service doesn't have to be expensive or grand; it can be something simple. Finally, I concluded by reiterating my love for Christmas.

What Should You Do?

Here are a few questions to help readers determine when to script and when not to for a sacrament meeting talk:

1. How comfortable are you with public speaking? If you tend to get nervous or lose your train of thought, scripting might be helpful to keep you on track.

1. How familiar are you with the topic? If you have a deep understanding and knowledge of the subject, you may not need a full script and can rely on an outline or notes.
2. How long is your talk? If it's a short talk (10-15 minutes), a well-organized outline or notes may be sufficient, whereas a longer talk might benefit from a complete script to ensure all points are covered.

3. How much time do you have to prepare? If you have limited time, focusing on creating a clear outline or notes could be more efficient than writing a full script. On the other hand, if you have ample time, scripting could help you refine your message and delivery.

4. What is your personal speaking style? Some people excel at delivering scripted talks, while others are more engaging and natural when speaking from an outline or notes. Consider which approach suits your style best.

Remember that in sacrament meetings, there are no slide shows or other types of presentations. Focus on the spoken word and make sure your message is clear, concise, and relevant to the audience.

Preparing to Deliver Your Talk

You've spent hours writing your talk, editing it again and again, and now the moment has arrived. You are about to deliver your talk in front of your ward for the very first time. To help you successfully deliver your talk, here are some strategic considerations that need to be made before you step up to the podium.

Here are my top tips on how to prepare to deliver your talk:

Timing is Crucial

As a speaker scheduled to deliver a sacrament talk, one of the key elements you need to consider is the importance of timing yourself and staying within the allotted time. This may seem like a minor detail, but it can have a significant impact on the effectiveness of your talk, the experience of the congregation, and the overall flow of the meeting.

Respecting the time allotted for your talk is a sign of respect for both the congregation and the meeting organizers. By staying within the time limit, you demonstrate that you value their time and attention. It shows that you have prepared your message thoughtfully and with consideration for the entire program. Moreover, it allows other speakers to have their fair share of time and ensures that the meeting doesn't run longer than planned, which could inconvenience the attendees.

Another important aspect of timing is maintaining the congregation's attention and interest. A well-timed talk can keep the audience engaged and receptive to the message you're sharing. On the other hand, a talk that runs too long may cause the congregation to lose focus, diminishing the impact of your message. By staying within your allotted time, you increase the likelihood that your message will be heard and remembered.

Additionally, adhering to the time limit helps with the overall pacing of the meeting. Sacrament meetings are carefully planned to ensure a smooth and cohesive flow, and each speaker's talk is a piece of the larger puzzle. When one talk runs too long, it can throw off the balance and disrupt the flow of the entire meeting. This can make it difficult for the congregation to fully absorb and appreciate each part of the program, as they may be preoccupied with concerns about the meeting running late or feeling rushed.

To ensure you stay within the allotted time, there are several strategies you can employ during your preparation and delivery:

1. Understand that when reading aloud, you will typically finish a standard US-Letter-sized page in about 2-3 minutes. This will give you a starting point when writing your talk.
2. Practice your talk multiple times aloud, timing yourself to see how long it takes to deliver. This will give you a realistic sense of the actual duration of your talk, allowing you to adjust your content accordingly.

1. Be mindful of your pacing while speaking. Speaking too quickly can make your talk feel rushed and may be difficult for the congregation to follow. On the other hand, speaking too slowly can cause your talk to drag on and potentially lose the audience's interest. Aim for a steady, natural pace that allows you to stay within the time limit without sacrificing clarity or impact.
2. Prioritize your content. If you find that your talk is running too long, consider what elements of your message are most crucial to convey. Focus on these key points and trim down or eliminate less essential parts of your talk.
3. Rehearse transitions between points, stories, and scriptures. Smooth transitions can help your talk flow more efficiently and

save time. Additionally, this practice will help you feel more confident and polished during your delivery.

4. Have a backup plan in case you find yourself running short or long during your actual talk. Prepare a few extra points or anecdotes that you can add if you need to fill time, or be prepared to gracefully wrap up your talk early if you're running long.

In conclusion, timing is a critical aspect of delivering an effective sacrament talk. By respecting the allotted time, you demonstrate your respect for the congregation, maintain their attention and interest, and contribute to the overall flow of the meeting. By practicing, prioritizing, and preparing, you can ensure that your talk is both impactful and well-timed.

Familiarize Yourself with the Chapel

Familiarizing yourself with the chapel's layout and podium is an essential step in preparing to deliver a talk in a sacrament meeting. By taking the time to become acquainted with the space where you will be speaking, you can alleviate some of the anxiety and uncertainty that often accompanies public speaking, especially for first-time speakers.

When you know the chapel's layout, you can better understand how your voice will carry through the room and determine the best way to engage with the congregation. This understanding allows you to make any necessary adjustments to your speaking volume, tone, or pacing to ensure that your message is clear and impactful. It's also an opportunity to identify any potential distractions, such as windows that may let in sunlight, and think about how to mitigate them during your talk.

The podium is an important focal point during your talk. It serves as a physical support and a space to place your notes or scriptures, so becoming familiar with its size, height, and design can help you feel more comfortable and confident when you step up to deliver your talk. Make sure to spend some time at the podium before your talk, adjusting the microphone if needed, and finding the best position for your notes.

By taking these steps to familiarize yourself with the chapel and the podium, you are better prepared to face the congregation with confidence and poise. This familiarity will help you concentrate on the message you want to share and connect with the audience, making your talk a more meaningful and inspiring experience for both you and the congregation. In the end, taking the time to understand the physical space where you will be speaking is a crucial aspect of delivering an impactful talk that leaves a lasting impression on your listeners.

Pray for Guidance

Praying for guidance and the Spirit to be with you during your talk is a vital aspect of preparing for a sacrament meeting. As a speaker, you have a unique opportunity to share insights and testimonies that can uplift and inspire the congregation. Inviting the Spirit to be present with you throughout your talk will allow you to share your message with greater clarity, power, and conviction.

Before your talk, take time to pray sincerely, asking Heavenly Father for guidance in delivering your message effectively. Pray for the ability to express your thoughts in a way that will resonate with your audience and for the courage to share your testimony with honesty and vulnerability. Praying for the Spirit's presence will also help to calm your nerves and provide comfort as you speak, knowing that you are not alone in this endeavor.

During your talk, you may feel prompted to share additional thoughts or experiences that come to your mind. Trust in these promptings, as they may be the very messages someone in the congregation needs to hear. Praying for the Spirit to guide your words will help you be more receptive to these divine promptings and enable you to deliver your talk with greater confidence and spiritual power.

Seeking guidance and inviting the Spirit to be with you as you speak will enhance your ability to communicate your message effectively and touch the hearts of those listening, leaving a lasting spiritual impact on their lives.

Hydration – Drink water, no carbonation or ice

Make sure that you stay hydrated before your talk by drinking a lot of water. Not only does water help you stay hydrated, but it also flushes out toxins and reduces bloat. Bloating can make you feel puffy and less confident.

You may want to bring a water bottle with you to your talk. Although it isn't appropriate to drink at the podium, it may be acceptable to sip some water before you stand up to speak.

Avoid carbonated beverages. If you are a soda drinker like I am, you probably know what happens when you drink them. That's right, gas. The urge to belch becomes almost overwhelming, which is not something you want to be doing in the middle of your talk.

Empty Your Pockets

Nothing can distract you or your audience more than a bunch of jingling keys or change in your pockets. Make sure you don't have anything in your pockets before you start your talk. You don't want them to fall out and distract you or your audience.

This was my number one weakness for many years. If there any of those objects in my pocket, I would subconsciously reach in and grab them. I was entirely unaware I was doing it until a friend pointed it out to me.

Now I make sure my pockets are always empty before I begin any type of talk or presentation.

Silence Your Devices

Besides the fact that it is incredibly rude to your audience to be on your phone, social media, or any kind of device during your talk, do you know how distracting your device's notifications are to you?

You may think you can manage the interruptions, but the truth is, you can't ignore notifications like text messages, emails, and social media posts. Instead, you'll find yourself getting distracted by them and losing your train of thought. If you must have your phone on you during your talk, turn it to silent so you don't get interrupted by notifications. Consider setting it to "Do Not Disturb" mode for the duration of your talk, so you don't get distracted by them.

A note on smart watches

There was a video circulating a while ago showing the President of the United States checking his watch repeatedly during an otherwise somber occasion. It wasn't a good look, and his political opponents lambasted him for it.

Now that I have a smartwatch myself, I think I understand. It is nearly impossible to resist looking at it when it vibrates, regardless of what else is going on. For this reason alone, I recommend removing it completely. If you don't want to do that, at least set it to "Do Not Disturb" until your talk is over.

Body Language

Good posture and body language are essential components of effective communication, particularly during a sacrament meeting talk. As you stand before the congregation, your body language can convey confidence, openness, and sincerity, which will help you connect with your audience and make your message more impactful.

To practice good posture, stand tall with your feet shoulder-width apart, and distribute your weight evenly between both legs. Keep your shoulders relaxed and pulled back slightly and engage your core muscles to maintain an upright posture. This stance not only projects confidence but also helps to maintain a steady breathing pattern, which is crucial for delivering your talk with clarity and control.

Don't cross your arms across your chest or place your hands in your pockets (see above about the keys). This is a defensive posture that doesn't project confidence or authority. Instead, keep your hands open, palms facing toward the audience. This will help you appear more approachable and confident.

Additionally, use hand gestures purposefully and naturally to emphasize points and convey emotion. However, be mindful not to overuse gestures, as excessive movement can be distracting. Strive for a balance that complements your words without detracting from your message.

As you practice and refine your posture and body language, you'll notice that your delivery becomes more polished, and your message resonates more profoundly with your audience.

Remember, your body language is a powerful tool in communication, and when used effectively, it can enhance your talk and create a memorable experience for those listening. Taking the time to practice and develop these skills will contribute to the overall effectiveness of your talk and leave a lasting impression on your audience.

Breathe

Breathing plays a crucial role in public speaking, including when delivering a sacrament meeting talk. Taking slow, deep breaths before your talk can help calm nerves, reduce anxiety, and improve focus. As you step up to the podium, remember to continue practicing mindful breathing throughout your speech.

During your talk, maintaining steady and controlled breathing will aid in delivering your message with clarity, confidence, and poise. Proper breathing also helps regulate your speaking pace, ensuring that your words flow naturally and coherently. By focusing on your breath, you can remain present, connected to the Spirit, and fully engaged with your audience, making your talk more impactful and inspiring.

Delivering Your Talk

As you stand ready to deliver your talk, remember that the key to success is simply stepping up and giving it your best effort. In public speaking, there are no true mistakes, only opportunities for growth and learning. It's natural to make errors during your speech, but rather than dwelling on them, embrace them as part of the journey towards becoming a better speaker. The most effective way to improve your public speaking skills is through consistent practice and courageously sharing your knowledge and insights with others. So go forth and let your voice be heard, knowing that each experience is a stepping stone towards greater confidence and impact.

Begin with a Central Theme

As you start the first section of your sacrament talk, it's crucial to establish a central theme that captures the essence of your message. This central theme serves to focus the attention of your ward members and helps prepare them for attentive listening.

A central theme is a concise summary of your entire sacrament talk. It should inform your audience about the subject matter, what they can anticipate hearing, and why it is relevant to them. This theme is a vital component of your talk, as it guides you while writing and assists you in delivering your message with clarity.

Naturally, your central theme can be a bit more elaborate than just a few words. Keep it succinct for clarity and let your audience know what they can expect. This theme should be a natural extension of the key points you want to convey, and it's what your listeners should remember after your talk concludes.

Avoid merely stating your topic; I will discuss this further in the section on what not to do. A well-crafted central theme can save you from potential pitfalls, making you appear thoughtful and organized since you have clearly considered the most effective way to present your topic. It can also help you organize your thoughts as you condense your entire talk into a single guiding statement.

Create a central theme that is three to five sentences long. The first sentence should include the topic you are discussing and inform your audience about what they will learn. The following sentences should highlight the specific insights they can expect to gain. The final sentence should explain why this information matters to them and how your talk will enrich their spiritual lives.

Begin with a Story

Alternatively, starting your sacrament talk with a story that connects to your central theme is an engaging and effective way to capture your audience's attention. Many General Authorities use this technique in their General Conference addresses, as stories help illustrate the principles they wish to teach and create a personal connection with the audience.

Sharing a story enables you to present your theme in a relatable and memorable manner, allowing your listeners to visualize the message you are conveying. Anecdotes can evoke emotions, generate interest, and encourage your audience to reflect on their own experiences, fostering a deeper understanding of the spiritual insights you wish to share.

As you begin your talk, choose a story that is relevant and meaningful to your central theme. Ensure that it resonates with your audience and supports the key points you want to make. Remember to keep the story concise and focused on the message you want to convey.

Stay on Topic and Avoid Tangents

While giving a sacrament talk, it's essential to remain focused and stay on topic. Have you ever listened to someone delivering a talk or presentation, only to witness them veering off into a seemingly unrelated tangent? This can be likened to the "Great Pumpkin monologue" from the Peanuts cartoons, where Linus suddenly shifts from his original topic to discuss the Great Pumpkin. As a speaker, it's crucial to avoid such digressions and maintain your audience's attention.

Straying from your topic can confuse your audience and dilute the impact of your message. It may also create an impression of disorganization, causing listeners to lose interest and question the relevance of your talk. Moreover, going off on tangents could lead to exceeding your allotted time, which might disrupt the flow of the meeting and inconvenience other speakers.

Some speakers struggle with the fear of silence, feeling compelled to fill every moment with words. However, it's essential to recognize that saying fewer, focused words is more powerful than filling the space with irrelevant content. To avoid rambling or deviating from your subject, practice focus and discipline in your preparation and delivery.

If you find yourself prone to going off on tangents, especially when nervous, have a few relevant points or stories prepared that you can use to refocus your talk. This will help you redirect your thoughts back to the central theme and ensure that your message remains clear and concise.

To prevent rambling, try these strategies:

1. Relax and turn off your inner critic. Trust in your preparation and the guidance of the Spirit.

1. If you've scripted your talk, consider marking your place as you

proceed through it. This will help you maintain your focus and stay on track.

2. Embrace brief moments of silence. Pauses can give you and your audience time to absorb the message and reflect on its significance.

By staying on topic and avoiding tangents, you'll deliver a more impactful and meaningful sacrament talk that will engage your listeners and leave a lasting impression.

Speak Slowly, Clearly, and Audibly

When delivering a sacrament talk, it's crucial to speak slowly, clearly, and audibly to ensure your audience can understand your message. Rushing through your talk may give listeners the impression that you're uncertain or nervous.

It's common for speakers to mumble when they're anxious. If you notice yourself becoming nervous, take a moment to pause at the end of a paragraph, breathe deeply, and start the next paragraph slowly and clearly. Mumbling can make your message difficult to understand, potentially leading to confusion or disinterest among your audience.

Speaking too softly is another common mistake. While it's not necessary to shout, your voice should be loud enough to be heard throughout the room. To project your voice, stand up straight, pull your shoulders back, and hold your head up. Remember, the more nervous or important the occasion, the louder you should speak.

Practicing your talk beforehand can help you gauge the appropriate volume. Consider recording yourself speaking a few paragraphs at the back of the room and playing it back to check the volume. Adjust as needed and enlist a partner to help if possible.

Avoid filler words like "like" or "um," which can indicate that you're searching for your next thought. Slowing down and taking your time will help you eliminate most of these problems.

If you're using a PA system, which you should be if you're in the chapel, position the microphone approximately 10-12 inches from your mouth. Speak clearly and confidently but leave the volume adjustments to those conducting the meeting.

By speaking slowly, clearly, and audibly during your sacrament talk, you'll effectively communicate your message and create a more engaging and spiritually uplifting experience for your audience.

The Awkward Pause

One of the challenges that some speakers face is dealing with awkward pauses. I have personally experienced this issue, and I'd like to share my story to help you understand how to handle such situations in a sacrament talk.

Sometimes, while speaking, I might forget the next word or the conclusion to the point I'm trying to make. For instance, I might say, "And if you do this well, you'll quickly see that..." and then draw a blank. This can create an awkward pause that may disrupt the flow of the talk.

To overcome this in a sacrament talk, I've found it helpful to have my conclusion statement written in my notes. This way, if I lose my train of thought, I can quickly glance at my notes and pick up where I left off. Having your thoughts organized and clear notes can greatly help you in maintaining the flow of your talk.

In situations where an awkward pause still occurs, it's essential to remain composed and take a brief moment to collect your thoughts. You can use this time to take a deep breath, regain your focus, and calmly continue with your talk. It's crucial to remember that everyone experiences moments like these, and it's entirely normal.

In a different setting, such as a Sunday School lesson, it may be appropriate to engage the audience or use visual aids like slides to help you remember key points. However, in a sacrament talk, it's best to rely on your prepared notes and composure to overcome these moments.

Overcoming awkward pauses in sacrament talks not only helps you deliver a more coherent and impactful message but also enables you to maintain a spiritual atmosphere and connect with your audience. By using these strategies, you can confidently share your insights and testimony without losing the flow of your talk.

Make Eye Contact

Establishing a connection with your audience is vital when delivering a sacrament talk, and one effective way to achieve this is through eye contact. By maintaining eye contact, you create a sense of engagement and sincerity, helping your listeners to feel more connected to your message.

As you begin your talk, scan the room and identify a few friendly faces. Aim for around five individuals, if possible. As you progress through your speech, shift your gaze between your notes and these people, making sure to include others in the audience as well. This method allows you to maintain a personal connection with your listeners while staying focused on your content.

Remember that the goal is to communicate directly with your audience, so be sure to address them rather than the horizon or an empty spot in the room. Use appropriate gestures and body language to reinforce your message but keep it natural and relevant to the context of your talk.

If you find it challenging to make direct eye contact with individuals in the audience, you can try an alternative approach. Look towards the back of the room, just above the heads of those seated in the last row. From the perspective of most audience members, it will appear as though you are making eye contact with people behind them. Although this method is not as effective as making direct eye contact, it can still help to create a sense of connection.

Making eye contact during your sacrament talk is crucial for fostering a sense of engagement and rapport with your audience. By looking directly at your listeners and occasionally focusing on specific individuals, you show that you are genuinely interested in sharing your testimony and insights with them. This, in turn, encourages your audience to be more receptive to your message, leading to a more meaningful and impactful sacrament talk.

Audience Feedback

Audience participation can be an effective way to engage listeners and encourage interaction in various settings, such as Sunday School lessons, youth activities, or even professional presentations. However, it is essential to understand that audience participation is generally not appropriate during sacrament meetings. In these settings, talks should be focused on sharing testimonies, insights, and spiritual messages without actively seeking input from the congregation.

That being said, it is crucial to be mindful of when and how to ask for audience feedback in other contexts. While involving the audience can enhance a lesson or presentation, it's important not to overuse this technique. Many speakers make the mistake of asking too many questions that require a response, which can become distracting or even frustrating for listeners.

In certain situations, asking rhetorical questions can be appropriate during a sacrament talk. Rhetorical questions can help to engage the audience mentally and encourage reflection on the topic without requiring an actual response. However, it's essential to use them sparingly and avoid overloading your talk with too many, which may lose their impact.

In a classroom or professional setting, it is usually acceptable to ask the audience to raise their hands or respond to questions. For instance, you might inquire who among the participants is familiar with the topic being discussed. However, asking more than two or three questions in a single presentation can be excessive, and many audience members may disengage or stop responding.

As a speaker or teacher, it's essential to strike a balance between engaging your audience and overwhelming them with excessive participation requests or rhetorical questions. Remember that the primary goal is to share your message effectively and inspire your listeners, so be mindful of how you involve them in the conversation.

Do Not Ask the Audience to Look Up Definitions

During sacrament meetings, it is not appropriate to ask the audience to look up definitions or scriptures. This type of engagement is better suited for other types of lessons, such as Sunday School or youth activities, where interaction and discussion are encouraged. As I've said, your focus should be on sharing your testimony, insights, and spiritual messages without requiring the congregation to perform tasks or provide feedback.

Asking the audience to look up definitions or scriptures during a talk can be seen as a delaying tactic. Some speakers who lack sufficient material may resort to this method to ease the pressure on themselves. However, this approach can cause the audience to lose focus and disengage from the speaker's message.

Instead of involving the audience in these tasks, it's better to prepare adequately for your talk by including relevant definitions, scriptures, or other resources in your presentation beforehand. If you are concerned that your talk may not have enough content, invest time in researching and developing additional material to enrich your message.

Remember that sacrament talks should maintain a spiritual focus and avoid asking the audience to perform tasks. Engaging the audience in this way is more appropriate in other lesson settings where active participation and discussion are expected.

By preparing well and delivering a focused, meaningful message, you can ensure that your sacrament talk resonates with your listeners and inspires them on their spiritual journey.

Do Not Use Long, Irrelevant Quotes with No Additional Analysis

Using relevant quotes can add a lot of power and authority to your talk. Some people make the mistake of using really long quotes, and never bridge the gap with their audiences as to its relevance.

This is a surefire way of losing your audience's attention.

Before deciding to include a particular quote in your talk or presentation, ask yourself:

- Is this directly relevant to the point you're making?
- Is it short enough that it won't distract from the main point of your talk?
- Is it a quote or is it really a story?

- If it's a quote, you'll want to make sure you attribute it properly.

It isn't enough to quote someone; you must tie it back to your topic. Make sure you add a paragraph or two, or a sentence or two, that explains why that information is useful and important to your topic.

The key to using a quote is not simply to repeat it, but to extrapolate the quote and apply it to your own ideas. Also, be sure to add your own analysis of the quote. This will make your talk more immediate and engaging to the audience.

Tell Relevant Stories

Humans are innately drawn to stories. We find meaning, connection, and inspiration through the narratives we share with each other, whether they are delivered through books, movies, TV shows, or spoken words. A well-told story can capture an audience's attention and make your message resonate more deeply.

When incorporating stories into your sacrament talk, it is crucial to ensure that they are relevant to your topic. As we just discussed, an unrelated story might be entertaining, but it can detract from the spiritual message you are trying to convey. By choosing a story that directly relates to your central theme, you can create a powerful and engaging connection with your audience.

One effective strategy is to include stories in your talk that illustrates the spiritual principle you are discussing. This approach can draw your audience in emotionally and set the stage for the insights and lessons you will share.

For example, in April 2003 General Conference, Elder Richard G. Scott shared this story.

Years ago I participated in the measurement of the nuclear characteristics of different materials. The process used an experimental nuclear reactor designed so that high energy particles streamed from a hole in the center of the reactor. These particles were directed into an experimental chamber where measurements were made. The high energy particles could not be seen, but they had to be carefully controlled to avoid harm to others. One day a janitor entered while we were experimenting. In a spirit of disgust he said, "You are all liars, pretending that you are doing something important, but you can't fool me. I know that if you can't see, hear, taste, smell, or touch it, it doesn't exist." That attitude ruled out the possibility of his learning that there is much of worth that can't be identified by the five senses. Had that man been willing to open his mind to understand how the presence of nuclear particles is detected, he would have confirmed their existence. In like manner, never doubt the reality of faith. You will gather the fruits of faith as you follow the principles God has established for its use.

Elder Scott used this story to teach about faith, which can also not be seen directly.

The story is concise, directly related to the message of his talk, and provides a powerful example of faith. This personal experience not only makes the talk more engaging but also helps the audience relate to the spiritual principle being taught.

Stories can greatly enhance your sacrament talk when used thoughtfully and with purpose. Make sure to choose stories that are relevant and directly connected to your topic, which will allow you to create a meaningful and memorable experience for your audience.

Avoid Overused Stories

While stories can serve as powerful tools in your sacrament talk, it is important to be mindful of the ones you choose to share. Some stories have been repeated so often that they have become clichés, and people have grown weary of hearing them. Sharing an overused story may have the unintended consequence of causing listeners to lose interest or disengage from your message.

To avoid this pitfall, be cautious about including stories that are too familiar or that have been recounted time and time again. Examples of such stories are:

- Footprints in the Sand
- The Boy Who Cried "Wolf"
- Alice meeting the Cheshire Cat in Alice in Wonderland
- The boy and the starfish on the beach

Before sharing a story, ask someone you trust about their familiarity with it. If you suspect that it may be well-known, consider finding a fresh angle or perspective to bring new life to the tale. Alternatively, seek out an entirely different story that will resonate with your listeners.

If you've got stories from your life, share them. The most impactful stories often come from your own life and experiences. These personal anecdotes are unique to you and are unlikely to have been heard before by your audience. By drawing from your own journey, you can share genuine, heartfelt moments that will engage and inspire those listening to your talk.

Ultimately, the key to a successful sacrament talk is to use stories that are relevant, authentic, and emotionally resonant. By being mindful of the stories you choose to share, you can create a meaningful and memorable experience for your audience, leaving them with insights and inspiration to carry with them in their own lives.

Finish in the Time Assigned

The length of your talk is an important aspect to consider, as it can impact not only your message but also the overall flow of the sacrament meeting. Although we've touched on this topic earlier, it's worth reiterating the importance of managing the duration of your talk.

Being mindful of the time allotted for your talk is a matter of courtesy and respect for both the audience and fellow speakers. If you have been assigned a 10-minute talk, sticking to that time frame ensures that other speakers have their fair share of time to share their messages. Going significantly shorter or longer than your allotted time can cause disruptions to the meeting's schedule.

In general, it's better to finish slightly under time rather than going over. If you have a 10-minute talk and finish in 8 minutes, it's acceptable; however, ending in just 3 minutes could make the next speaker feel rushed or pressured to fill in the extra time.

By being conscious of your talk's duration and making an effort to stay within the time constraints, you contribute to a smooth and well-organized sacrament meeting that respects the efforts of both the audience and your fellow speakers.

Practice Your Talk

The importance of practicing your talk cannot be overstated, as it's a crucial step in delivering a well-prepared and engaging message. To ensure your talk is as effective as possible, invest time and effort into rehearsing it.

Practicing your talk aloud allows you to become familiar with the content, and it helps you gauge the duration of your presentation. By timing yourself, you can make necessary adjustments to fit within the allotted time frame. Additionally, rehearsing in front of a trusted friend or family member can provide valuable feedback and suggestions for improvement.

Recording your practice sessions can be an enlightening experience. Watching the recording after a short break can help you identify areas for improvement, such as fidgeting, talking too fast, or speaking too softly. Observing your own performance provides a unique perspective and can reveal habits or mannerisms that might be distracting to your audience.

By consistently practicing your talk, you build confidence, refine your delivery, and ensure that your message is effectively communicated to your audience. This preparation will contribute to a more polished and engaging presentation during the sacrament meeting.

Concluding Your Talk

As you approach the end of your talk, it's essential to leave a lasting impression on your audience and reinforce the main message. Here are some steps to help you wrap up your talk effectively in sacrament meetings:

1. Restate Your Topic: By the conclusion of your talk, your audience should have a clear understanding of your topic. However, it's still important to explicitly restate your theme or central idea. This reinforces the message and ensures it's fresh in their minds as they leave the meeting.

1. Summarize Your Key Points: Throughout your talk, you've likely shared several valuable insights related to your topic. To strengthen the impact of your message, briefly summarize these

points in a concise and organized manner. This repetition helps solidify the information in the minds of your listeners and highlights the main takeaways from your talk.

2. Share a Final Thought or Personal Testimony: To create a memorable and meaningful conclusion, consider sharing a final thought, a personal experience, or your testimony related to the topic. This emotional and personal touch can leave a lasting impact and inspire your audience to reflect on what they've learned.

3. Express Gratitude: Before ending your talk, take a moment to express gratitude for the opportunity to speak and to your audience for their attention and engagement. This gesture shows your appreciation and fosters a sense of community and connection.

Elder David A. Bednar of the Quorum of the Twelve Apostles delivered a talk titled "Bear Up Their Burdens with Ease" during the April 2014 General Conference. In this talk, Elder Bednar effectively employs most of the steps mentioned earlier in concluding his message.

1. He restates his topic, which focuses on how the Atonement of Jesus Christ helps us bear our burdens with ease.

1. Elder Bednar summarizes his key points, including understanding the Savior's Atonement and the enabling power of His grace.

2. He shares his testimony and a final thought on the importance of coming unto Christ and finding strength and support through His Atonement.

By following these steps, you can effectively wrap up your sacrament meeting talk, leaving your audience with a memorable message and a lasting impression.

Analyzing the "Worst Talk"

Remember that "worst talk" from the beginning of the book? I want to go through it here and discuss why it was so bad, beyond the obvious.

For context, I wrote this talk with the intention of breaking as many of my rules as possible.

The text of the talk is in *italics* and my commentary is not. Some of the commentary is identical to what I included previously in the book but presented again alongside the example.

So, let's start.

Audience Interaction

Good morning, folks. [If no one responds, repeat it until you get a response.] For those of you who don't know me, my name is ________________ and have been in this ward for the past year.

There are a few problems with the opening of the "worst sacrament talk." First, it is somewhat informal, which is not ideal for sacrament meetings. It's essential to maintain a reverent and respectful tone throughout the talk. Second, sacrament talks are not meant to be interactive. Attempting to elicit responses from the congregation is unnecessary and can be distracting.

Introducing yourself in sacrament meeting is generally not required, as the person conducting the meeting usually introduces the speakers. Repeating the introduction wastes time and detracts from the main focus of the talk, which is to share a spiritual message. If you feel the need to introduce yourself, keep it brief and focus on your name and, if applicable, your role in the ward or church.

Remember, the congregation is present to hear an uplifting message, not to engage in a back-and-forth conversation or listen to extensive personal introductions. Maintaining a reverent and focused atmosphere will ensure a more effective and inspiring sacrament meeting talk.

Humor

*Today I intend for my talk to be like a ghostly elevator——it
will lift your spirits! [Chuckle at your own horrible joke]*

Opening a sacrament meeting talk with a joke can be risky, as humor may not be suitable for the reverent and spiritual atmosphere of the meeting. It's essential to be cautious when considering using humor in a talk, as it can be difficult to get right and can potentially offend someone in the congregation. In most cases, it's better to focus on delivering an uplifting and spiritually engaging message.

If you still feel inclined to incorporate humor into your talk, make sure to practice your delivery and timing with someone who can provide honest feedback. Keep in mind that sacrament meetings are meant to be spiritual and uplifting, so ensure that any humor you include is respectful and aligns with the purpose of the meeting.

Additionally, avoid using self-deprecating humor at the beginning of your talk, as it can diminish your credibility and impact as a speaker. Instead, focus on sharing a personal experience or story that relates to your topic and helps create a meaningful connection with the congregation.

Is humor always inappropriate? Not at all. You simply need to be careful.

Announcing Your Topic

The bishop asked me to speak for five minutes on faith.

In a sacrament meeting, it is not necessary to explicitly announce the topic of your talk in advance. Instead, let your content and message convey the topic naturally. Start your talk with an engaging opening paragraph that indirectly introduces the subject matter, allowing your audience to grasp the theme as you progress.

If the sacrament meeting has been well-planned, attendees will already have an understanding of the general theme or focus of the meeting. The specific details of your talk, however, should unfold organically during your presentation.

Instead of announcing the topic, consider beginning with a relevant scripture, personal experience, or story that connects to your message. This approach will engage your listeners and help them become emotionally invested in your talk.

As you proceed, the central theme will become clear to your audience without the need for a direct announcement. By doing so, you create a more meaningful and memorable experience for your listeners.

Questioning Your Selection

I don't know why the Bishop thought I was the right person to speak on faith. I spent most of the week trying to get out of it, but I didn't do a very good job, so here I am.

It is normal for speakers to experience self-doubt or question their suitability for a particular topic when asked to give a sacrament talk. This feeling, often known as "impostor syndrome," is common among individuals addressing an audience during church meetings. However, it is important not to express these doubts publicly during your talk, as doing so can create a negative impression and set an expectation of failure among your listeners.

Instead, focus on delivering a well-prepared and relevant talk that reflects your understanding and perspective on the gospel topic. To accomplish this, keep the following suggestions in mind:

1. Accept speaking assignments on topics you feel comfortable discussing. While you don't need to be an expert, ensure you have enough knowledge and background to provide a meaningful and informed perspective.

2. Thoroughly research and understand your material. Invest time in studying the topic, reviewing relevant scriptures, and seeking insights from General Authorities or other reliable sources.

3. Share personal experiences, stories, or testimonies that relate to the subject. These unique perspectives will make your talk engaging and relatable.

4. Embrace your role as a speaker during sacrament meeting and recognize that you have valuable insights to share. Remember that your perspective is important, and your ward members will appreciate your sincere effort to enlighten and uplift them.

5. Avoid displaying speaker notes or expressing uncertainty during your talk. Instead, exude confidence and maintain eye contact with your audience.

6. Trust in the guidance of the Holy Ghost. As you seek inspiration and pray for assistance, you will be directed in your preparation and delivery, ensuring your message resonates with your listeners.

Elder Neal A. Maxwell, a former member of the Quorum of the Twelve Apostles, once addressed this in an article published in the July 1975 Ensign magazine, titled "It's Service, Not Status, That Counts."

"God does not begin by asking about our ability, but only about our availability, and if we then prove our dependability, he will increase our capability."

It is a wonderful reminder that the Lord focuses on our willingness to serve and our dedication to fulfilling our assignment, rather than our pre-existing abilities.

Keep these things in mind. You will find that you can overcome self-doubt and deliver an impactful and inspiring sacrament talk, regardless of the topic.

Complaining About the Talk

I hate giving talks so I put this off till this afternoon, so hopefully the Spirit will be here to teach you something.

One of the least helpful things you can do in your sacrament talk is to tell the congregation that you don't want to be speaking to them. It is not only inappropriate but also counterproductive for the spiritual atmosphere.

Furthermore, complaining about giving the talk sets the wrong tone and communicates to everyone that you don't want to be there and likely didn't prepare well. Giving a sacrament talk is a significant responsibility and should be treated with reverence.

If you genuinely feel that you cannot give the talk, it is better to discuss your concerns with your church leaders beforehand. However, if you have accepted the invitation to speak, take responsibility for your commitment. While it's natural to be nervous, trust that you will be guided and supported.

If you find yourself in a situation where you didn't choose to give a talk but have no other choice, remember that the guidance provided in this discussion can help you get through it. Who knows? You might discover that you enjoy sharing your insights and testimony with the congregation after all.

Apologizing Ahead of Time

I apologize for this talk's poor quality. I was too bogged down with my video games and band to even consider doing this.

In a sacrament meeting, it's crucial to avoid apologizing for your talk's perceived poor quality. When you express that you're not as prepared as you'd like to be or provide reasons for why your talk might not be engaging, you undermine your own efforts and diminish the spiritual experience for the congregation.

Perhaps you didn't have enough time to prepare or feel less familiar with the material than you would prefer. Despite these challenges, it's essential not to dwell on them during your talk. Most people in the congregation will not notice whether you've prepared as much as you'd like. They are there to feel the Spirit and learn from your insights and testimony.

Remember that members of the congregation understand that giving a talk can be nerve-wracking. They will generally empathize with you, giving you the benefit of the doubt. They know that public speaking can be uncomfortable and will often forgive any mistakes or imperfections you might have.

By announcing your perceived shortcomings ahead of time, you set yourself up to fail and potentially detract from the spiritual atmosphere of the meeting. Instead, focus on the positive aspects of your message, trust in the guidance of the Spirit, and do your best to share your insights and testimony with humility and sincerity.

False Gratitude

Even so, I am grateful for the opportunity for me to get up to speak to you today. Talks are supposed to be a great opportunity for y'all to learn from me, but I definitely learned more writing this talk.

While it is true that you will probably learn your topic more deeply by preparing for a talk, you need not mention it. I have heard people say this often enough that it seems to be a common trope, which you are better off avoiding entirely.

When giving a sacrament talk, you might instead consider focusing on expressing gratitude for the opportunity to share your insights and testimony with the congregation. You can acknowledge that preparing for the talk has been a valuable experience and helped you grow spiritually, but it's essential to maintain a humble and sincere tone.

For example, you could say, "I am grateful for the opportunity to stand before you today and share my thoughts on this important topic. As I prepared for this talk, I gained new insights and deepened my understanding of the gospel principles. My hope is that the thoughts and experiences I share today will be a blessing to all of us and help us draw closer to our Heavenly Father."

By focusing on the shared learning experience and spiritual growth, you create a more inclusive and uplifting atmosphere for your sacrament talk.

Definitions

According to Google, the definition of faith is "complete trust or confidence in someone or something", which is far more accurate than the definition of faith as given by Abbott's Webster Selected

Dictionary circa 1923 which says that faith is "complete coincidence."

Starting your sacrament talk with a dictionary or Google definition of your topic can come across as uninspired and unoriginal. Relying on such definitions might give the impression that you haven't invested the time or effort to delve deeper into the subject matter or develop a more engaging introduction.

Instead of using a generic definition, consider crafting a more compelling opening that captures your audience's attention and connects with them on a personal level. Share a brief, relevant anecdote or personal experience that relates to the topic and sets the tone for your talk. This approach not only helps establish rapport with the congregation but also adds depth and authenticity to your message.

If you've previously given a talk on a similar topic and used a story that resonated with the audience, it's acceptable to reuse that story, as long as it remains relevant and impactful. Aim to keep your opening anecdote around two minutes in length. While it's possible to extend the story slightly, be cautious about exceeding three minutes, as your audience may start to lose interest or become restless.

By opting for a more engaging and personal introduction, you demonstrate your genuine commitment to the topic and create a meaningful connection with your listeners, setting the stage for a successful sacrament talk.

Irrelevant Tangents

To demonstrate my tremendous faith, I'd like to say a few words about the Great Pumpkin. Halloween will soon be with us, and on Halloween night, the Great Pumpkin rises out of the pumpkin patch, and brings toys to all the good little children. I have complete confidence, or faith, that, on Halloween night, the Great Pumpkin will be there. You'll see. You'll all see. I'll be there ready to meet him when he comes. None of you have the faith that I do in the Great Pumpkin.

If y'all turn to 2 Chronicles 12:3-7—go ahead, I'll wait. ... ... Are we all there? (Repeat if no response) Yes? Good. Going on. In 2 Chronicles 12:3-7, it reads "With twelve hundred chariots, and threescore thousand horsemen: and the people were without number that came with him out of Egypt; the Lubims, the Sukkiims, and the Ethiopians. And he took the fenced cities which pertained to Judah, and came to Jerusalem.

Then came Shemaiah the prophet to Rehoboam, and to the princes of Judah, that were gathered together to Jerusalem because of Shishak, and said unto them, Thus saith the Lord, Ye have forsaken me, and therefore have I also left you in the hand of Shishak. Whereupon the princes of Israel and the king humbled themselves; and they said, The Lord is righteous." Think about that next time you lack faith.

It is crucial to avoid irrelevant tangents and scripture references that don't directly connect to the topic of your sacrament talk. Straying from your subject matter can lead to confusion and disengagement from your audience. While stories, analogies, and metaphors can be powerful tools in drawing your listeners closer to you, they must be relevant and complement the overall message you aim to convey.

Although there may be exceptional speakers who can skillfully weave seemingly unrelated stories into their talks, it is generally best to stay on topic to ensure clarity and coherence. Veering off on unrelated tangents can detract from your main points, dilute your message, and leave your audience feeling unsatisfied or perplexed.

For example, in the October 2009 General Conference, Elder David A. Bednar shared a story that seemed tangential at first but was eventually tied to his main message. He began by recounting his childhood experiences working on a farm, specifically the process of making hay and stacking bales. At first, this anecdote appeared unrelated to his topic, which was the Atonement of Jesus Christ.

However, as he continued, Elder Bednar drew a connection between the process of making hay and the spiritual principles he wanted to emphasize. He explained how the physical labor involved in hay-making had taught him about the importance of steady, consistent effort. He then connected this lesson to the process of spiritual growth, highlighting that we must continually and consistently rely on the Atonement of Jesus Christ to overcome our weaknesses and progress toward eternal life.

By initially sharing a seemingly unrelated story, Elder Bednar was able to engage his audience and eventually tie it back to his main message in a powerful and memorable way.

When incorporating stories, analogies, or metaphors in your talk, ensure they have a strong connection to your topic and effectively illustrate the principles you are discussing. These narrative elements should serve to enhance your message, not distract from it. As you prepare your talk, carefully evaluate each story or analogy to determine if it genuinely supports your intended message.

By maintaining focus on your topic and incorporating relevant and relatable stories, you can create a more engaging and meaningful sacrament talk. This approach allows you to forge a stronger connection with your listeners and help them better understand and internalize the spiritual truths you are sharing.

Overused and/or Irrelevant Stories

I would like to share with you a story I heard during some session of general conference recently from a General Authority and then again several times in sacrament meeting over the past few months. Most of you are familiar with Alice in Lewis Carroll's classic novel Alice's Adventures in Wonderland. You will remember that she comes to a crossroads with two paths before her, each stretching onward but in opposite directions. As she contemplates which way to turn, she is confronted by the Cheshire Cat, of whom Alice asks, "Which path shall I follow?" The cat answers, "That depends where you want to go. If you do not know where you want to go, it doesn't matter which path you take." That, my friends, takes real faith.

Using overused stories, such as the Alice in Wonderland meeting the Cheshire Cat anecdote, can be a drawback when giving a sacrament talk. While minor diversions and tangents can sometimes strengthen a talk, it is crucial to ensure that the stories you share are relevant and directly support your main topic.

When selecting a story, make sure it complements and enhances your message. If you find yourself needing to add lengthy explanations to connect the story to your topic, it may not be the best choice. A well-chosen story should require minimal explanation and should seamlessly contribute to the development of your talk.

When incorporating multiple stories in your talk, strive for coherence and balance. Ensure that the stories illustrate your main points and are relatively independent of each other. Avoid using interdependent stories, as they may detract from one another and weaken the overall impact of your message.

We have all encountered speakers who have shared stories that, while interesting, did not provide any valuable insight into the topic at hand. This often indicates that the speaker did not invest enough time and thought into selecting stories that truly resonate with the message they intend to convey.

As a speaker, you should strive to avoid falling into this trap. Thoughtfully choose stories that not only engage your audience but also meaningfully contribute to your message. By doing so, you will create a more powerful and memorable sacrament talk that will leave a lasting impression on your listeners.

Remember, your goal is to deliver a compelling and insightful talk that genuinely connects with your audience. Don't let overused or irrelevant stories detract from your message. Instead, focus on finding stories that truly enhance and support your main points, creating a strong and cohesive narrative.

Weak Conclusion

In conclusion, I'd like to bear my testimony that I know this church is true. In the name of thy son, Jesus Christ. Amen.

A strong conclusion is essential in creating a lasting impression on your audience and effectively summarizing your sacrament talk. The weak conclusion mentioned above does not achieve this goal, as it lacks thought and fails to recap the key points of the talk. It appears as though the speaker is merely trying to complete their task without putting in the effort required for a meaningful conclusion.

To create a powerful conclusion, focus on restating the main problem or point, and suggest an action or solution that your audience can apply in their lives. By restating your main points in a general way, you can remind your listeners of the primary message of your talk while drawing your presentation to a close.

When closing your talk in the name of Jesus Christ, it is important to remember that you are addressing the congregation and not offering a prayer. As such, avoid using terms like "thy son," which only makes sense in a prayer setting.

Moreover, avoid using phrases such as "I'd like to" when bearing your testimony. Certainly, a powerful testimony should be specific to the topic of your talk, connecting the principles you've discussed to your personal experiences and convictions.

Sharing a heartfelt testimony related to your subject matter can create a lasting impact on your audience, helping to reinforce your message and strengthen the faith of those listening.

Crafting a thoughtful and impactful conclusion is essential for your sacrament talk. By restating your main points, offering a solution or action for your audience, and expressing a sincere testimony, you can create a lasting impression and ensure that your message resonates with your listeners.

Remember, the conclusion is your final opportunity to leave a mark on your audience, so make it count by dedicating time and effort to create a meaningful and memorable ending to your talk.

Rewriting the Worst Talk

Sacrament Talk Mastery

Topic _Faith_   Date _Sept 10_

List three hynms
84 Faith of our Fathers
263 Go Forth with Faith
85 How Firm a Foundation ✔

Related Scriptures
Isaiah 41:10
Isaiah 43:2–5
Helaman 5:12 ✔

General Conference Talks, Videos, etc.
A Sure Foundation, Dean Davies, April 2013
Therefore They Hushed Their Fears, David A Bednar, April 2015 ✔
The Witness, Boyd K Packer, April 2014
Finding Lasting Peace and Building Eternal Families, L. Tom Perry, Oct 2014

Stories and Other Personal Experiences (just enough for you to remember them)
Story from conference about the boy afraid of the pool.
The story of my taking the job in Texas – Leap of faith

Create an outline of the above elements in order (Use the back if necessary)

Start with the dilemma of the job offer
Great job, but unknown city
Exciting but scary
prayer? Go for it? Leap or not?
Faith in the Lord is important when facing challenges
Tell Bednar GC story about boy and pool
Leaping into pool like taking a leap of faith

Describe how job offer was similar
What did we decide?
How did it turn out?
Testify of faith

Mention hymn?
Read Helaman 5:12?

Let's apply the quick recipe from earlier in the book to the "Worst talk" and see how that might look in practice. We'll start with the topic (faith) and work from there. Refer to the image as we go through the steps.

Sample Sacrament Talk Worksheet – Design by Author

Sample

Find a hymn on faith. A quick way to do that is to use the Gospel Library app (https://www.churchofjesuschrist.org/learn/mobile-applications/gospel-library).

For this example, let's choose #85, How Firm a Foundation.

This hymn lists three scripture references: Isaiah 41:10, Isaiah 43:2–5, Helaman 5:12. I selected the Helaman version, which reads as follows:

And now, my sons, remember, remember that it is upon the rock of our Redeemer, who is Christ, the Son of God, that ye must build your foundation; that when the devil shall send forth his mighty winds, yea, his shafts in the whirlwind, yea, when all his hail and his mighty storm shall beat upon you, it shall have no power over you to drag you down to the gulf of misery and endless wo, because of the rock upon which ye are built, which is a sure foundation, a foundation whereon if men build they cannot fall.

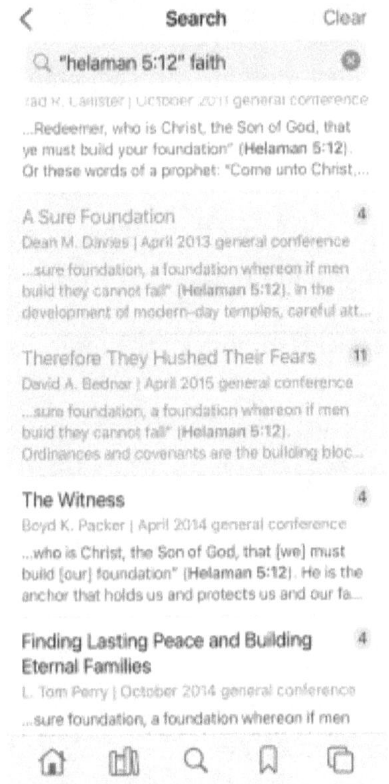

Next, we can search for that scripture in the Gospel Library app to find some conference talks. You could also do it at ChurchOfJesusChrist.org. For this discussion, assume we decided on "Therefore They Hushed Their Fears" by David A. Bednar from the April 2015 General Conference.

The next step is to come up with a personal experience where I had to exercise my own faith. I came up with one about moving to a new city to take a job. Your experience will be necessary for this step and the rest.

Next, connect all the elements into a single, cohesive narrative. This will obviously be different for everyone. In my case, I like starting with the story, and then explaining how it relates to the topic.

At this point, if you have reached the time allotted, you can simply express your gratitude (if that's what you want to express) about what you learned, shared, etc.

If you need to extend your talk to fit a longer time, repeat the above steps. For this example, I'm going to leave it here and not repeat.

And finally, conclude with your own personal testimony of the topic, its relevance to your life, and end.

Not the Worst Talk

Now let's see how it turned out. I don't promise perfection, but I hope you'll agree it's better than it was.

A few years ago, I was faced with a difficult decision. I had been offered a new job opportunity that was exciting, but it required me to move to a new city and leave behind the comfort of my current job and community. I was torn between the excitement of this new opportunity and the fear of the unknown.

As I prayed and sought guidance, I felt the Lord prompting me to take the leap and accept the new job offer. Despite my fear and uncertainty, I trusted that the Lord had a plan for me and that He would be with me every step of the way.

This experience reminded me of the importance of having faith in the Lord and trusting in His plan for us, even when we face difficult decisions and challenges. It is through our faith in Him that we can find strength, courage, and peace in this life.

Still, making such a life-altering chance can be scary, some might even say terrifying. Fortunately, exercising faith can quiet our fears.

Elder David A. Bednar spoke about this in his talk "Therefore They Hushed Their Fears" during the April 2015 General Conference. He shared a story about a young boy who was afraid to jump into the deep end of the pool. His father, sensing his fear, encouraged him to jump and promised to catch him. Despite his fear, the boy took the leap and felt his father catch him as promised.

In the same way, as we exercise faith and trust in our Heavenly Father, He catches us when we leap. He is always there to guide and support us through life's challenges and uncertainties.

Looking back on that moment, I realize that exercising faith and trusting in the Lord's plan for me was the best decision I ever made. Though I was afraid to take the leap and move to a new city, I felt the reassurance that the Lord was with me every step of the way. And as I exercised faith and trusted in Him, everything turned out great.

Elder Bednar's talk reminded me that as we exercise faith in our Heavenly Father, He catches us when we leap. The Lord blessed me with the courage and strength to take that leap of faith and move to a new city. He helped me find a new community, build new friendships, and grow both personally and professionally.

Through this experience, I have learned that when we put our faith in the Lord and trust in His plan for us, He is always there to guide and support us. As we exercise faith and take leaps of faith, the Lord blesses us with opportunities for growth and success beyond our imagination.

In closing, I testify that having faith in our Heavenly Father and building our lives upon the foundation of Christ is the surest way to find peace, comfort, and strength in this life. May we all strive to increase our faith and trust in the Lord each day. In His name, amen.

What do you think? Notice that I didn't quote from the hymn or the scripture reference I found. I could have. Maybe I should have. You can do so if you want.

Instead, I used those as part of my research. The topic led me to a hymn, which led me to a scripture, which led me to a conference talk, which led me to a story, which helped me remember a story from my own experience.

These things built on each other to help me craft a unique and personal sacrament talk, which covers the assigned topic, without resorting to any verbal crutches.

And I did it without breaking any of the rules.

If I needed to make the talk longer, I could easily have added more detail about the job, why it was a great opportunity, and why I was afraid to take it. I could have also used the same techniques to find other conference talks. I could have added more scripture references and hymns.

This quick and simple recipe gives you a framework you can use to craft your own effective and personal sacrament talk that your ward will remember.

Download the Worksheet

I have created a helpful resource to support you in crafting a great sacrament talk. It's a printable worksheet that follows the recipes we've discussed, making it easier for you to structure your talk effectively. This worksheet is designed to guide you through the process, step by step, ensuring that you cover all the essential elements of a successful talk. To access the worksheet, simply visit my website at https://walkingriver.gumroad.com/l/sacrament-worksheet. It's available for download, and you can print it out to use as a handy reference while preparing your talk. I hope this tool will be valuable in helping you deliver a meaningful and impactful message to your congregation.

Special Considerations

Preparing and giving a sacrament talk can be a daunting task for anyone, but for those with disabilities, mental health conditions, or social anxiety, it can be an especially challenging experience. In this chapter, we will explore some special considerations and strategies for making sacrament meeting talks more accessible and inclusive for all members.

It is important to recognize that not all members have the same abilities or opportunities to prepare and deliver a talk in sacrament meeting.

Section 38.8.27.4 of the General Handbook states that:

> *Leaders and teachers should include members with disabilities in meetings, classes, and activities as fully as possible. Lessons, talks, and teaching methods should be adapted to meet each person's needs.*

Let's explore some types of accommodations that might be made for individuals with extraordinary circumstances.

Disabilities

Members with disabilities may face unique challenges in preparing and delivering a sacrament talk. For example, those who are blind may have difficulty reading printed materials, while those who are deaf may have trouble listening to audio recordings. One solution for individuals with disabilities is to work with their bishop or other church leaders to find accommodations that will allow them to fully participate in the sacrament meeting. This may include the use of assistive technology or the assistance of a family member or friend.

In my ward, we have a sign language interpreter regularly attend our Sacrament Meeting from the other side of the country. Her assistance has been a major blessing for our one deaf member.

Mental Handicaps

Individuals with mental handicaps may have difficulty understanding and communicating complex ideas. In these cases, it may be helpful to simplify the topic and use concrete examples and visual aids to help illustrate key points. Additionally, it may be beneficial to work with a trusted family member, friend, or church leader who can provide support and guidance throughout the preparation process.

Social Anxiety

For individuals with social anxiety, the thought of speaking in front of a large group of people can be overwhelming. In these cases, it may be helpful to practice speaking in smaller groups or to seek support from a trusted friend or church leader. Additionally, it may be beneficial to choose a topic that is familiar and meaningful to the individual, as this can help to reduce anxiety and increase confidence.

Physically Unable to Attend

Another possible solution exists for individuals who are unable to physically attend sacrament meeting due to illness or being homebound. With the advancement of technology, remote speaking has become increasingly common and accessible.

Some individuals may feel more comfortable pre-recording their talk and playing it during the sacrament meeting, with the bishop's approval, of course.

Alternatively, they could also arrange for someone to read their talk on their behalf during the meeting, such as a trusted family member or friend. It is important to remember that while physical attendance is ideal, there are ways to accommodate and include individuals who may be unable to attend in person.

While it may not be a common occurrence, there is precedent for a speaker to give a talk on behalf of another person even at the highest levels of church leadership. A notable example is when President Thomas S. Monson opened the October 1989 General Conference by reading a talk that had been prepared by President Ezra Taft Benson. When circumstances arise that prevent someone from speaking in person, it is possible to have someone else deliver the message for them.

Language Barriers

Language barriers can be a significant challenge for those who do not speak the same language as the majority of the ward. In such cases, it may be challenging to convey your message effectively. However, it is still possible to prepare and deliver a meaningful talk.

One possible solution is to work with a translator who can help you translate your talk into the language of the congregation. This translator could be a member of the ward who is fluent in both languages or someone who is hired for the occasion.

My stake is a healthy mix of native-English and native-Spanish speakers. Our Stake Conferences usually consist of talks from both, with live translation.

Don't let unfamiliarity with the local language be a barrier for you.

Other Ailments

Individuals with other ailments, such as chronic pain or fatigue, may have difficulty finding the energy and focus to prepare and deliver a sacrament talk. In these cases, it may be helpful to prioritize self-care and to work with church leaders to find accommodations that will allow the individual to participate in the sacrament meeting in a way that is comfortable and meaningful. This may include the use of a chair or other seating accommodations, or the ability to participate remotely via video conferencing technology.

That's a Wrap!

I hope you enjoyed the book and that it has given you the knowledge and confidence you need to give an effective and inspiring sacrament meeting talk.

You've learned that the key to a good talk is to share personal experiences and gospel principles in a clear and simple way that connects with your audience. Your talk should inspire and uplift others, bringing them closer to Christ. We've also discussed the importance of prayer and the guidance of the Spirit as you prepare and deliver your talk.

To make your talk unique and engaging, we've discussed the importance of brainstorming creative ideas and using resources such as hymns, church magazines, and General Conference talks. These resources can add depth and variety to your message and make your talk more interesting and relevant to your audience.

We've also talked about how to deliver your talk effectively. This includes good pacing, vocal variety, and body language. It's important to be authentic and speak from the heart while also being mindful of your audience's needs and emotions.

It's also important to avoid common mistakes such as going over time, using inappropriate stories, and getting too caught up in your own thoughts and ideas.

Now it's time to take everything you've learned and go deliver a fantastic sacrament meeting talk. Rely on prayer and the Spirit as you prepare and deliver your message, and to speak from the heart with authenticity and sincerity. By following these guidelines, you'll be well on your way to delivering an effective, inspiring, and memorable talk that will uplift and inspire those around you.

A Simple Request

If I have offered even one piece of advice you find helpful, then I consider the effort of writing it as time well spent.

Please consider leaving me a positive review at the place where you purchased it. Also consider some of my other titles you find there.

Don't forget to download the Sacrament Talk Worksheet! It's a helpful tool that accompanies this book, guiding you through the process of creating an effective talk. Visit https://walkingriver.gumroad.com/l/sacrament-worksheet to access and download the worksheet. Happy speaking!

Do you have any advice about giving talks from your own experience? Share them with me. Feel free to email me with questions, stories, or comments at michael@walkingriver.com. Who knows? Your story might make it into my next book!

Please follow me at Twitter for regular updates. My handle is @walkingriver[1].

---

1. https://twitter.com/walkingriver

Talks and Articles Referenced

I referenced a number of talks delivered in General Conference and one magazine article as examples of techniques that should be emulated. These inspiring talks, delivered by church leaders and members, serve as powerful examples of effective and spiritually uplifting communication. As you explore these talks, you'll gain valuable insights into the art of delivering impactful sacrament talks while deepening your understanding of gospel principles and strengthening your testimony.

The talks below are listed in the order they appear in the book.

Elder Quentin L Cook. "Deep and Lasting Conversion to Heavenly Father and the Lord Jesus Christ." Saturday Morning Session, October 2018. https://www.churchofjesuschrist.org/study/general-conference/2018/10/deep-and-lasting-conversion-to-heavenly-father-and-the-lord-jesus-christ?lang=eng

President Thomas S. Monson. "Finding Joy in the Journey." Sunday Morning Session, October 2008. https://www.churchofjesuschrist.org/study/general-conference/2008/10/finding-joy-in-the-journey?lang=eng

Elder Joseph B. Wirthlin. "Come What May and Love It. Saturday Afternoon Session, October 2008. https://www.churchofjesuschrist.org/study/general-conference/2008/10/come-what-may-and-love-it?lang=eng

Elder Jeffrey R. Holland. "Like a Broken Vessel." Saturday Afternoon Session, October 2013. https://www.churchofjesuschrist.org/study/general-conference/2013/10/like-a-broken-vessel?lang=eng

President Thomas S. Monson. "The Priesthood – A Sacred Trust." Priesthood Session, April 1994. https://site.churchofjesuschrist.org/

study/general-conference/1994/04/the-priesthood-a-sacred-trust?lang=eng

President Dieter F. Uchtdorf. "Your Happily Ever After." General Young Women Meeting, April 2010. https://site.churchofjesuschrist.org/study/general-conference/2010/04/your-happily-ever-after?lang=eng

Elder Richard G. Scott. "The Sustaining Power of Faith in Times of Uncertainty and Testing." Sunday Morning Session, April 2003. https://site.churchofjesuschrist.org/study/general-conference/2003/04/the-sustaining-power-of-faith-in-times-of-uncertainty-and-testing

Elder David A. Bednar, "Bear Up Their Burdens with Ease." Sunday Morning Session, April 2014. https://www.churchofjesuschrist.org/study/general-conference/2014/04/bear-up-their-burdens-with-ease

Elder Neal A. Maxwell. "It's Service, Not Status, That Counts." April 1975 *Ensign.* https://www.churchofjesuschrist.org/study/ensign/1975/07/its-service-not-status-that-counts?lang=eng

Elder David A. Bednar. "More Diligent and Concerned at Home," Saturday Morning Session, October 2009. https://www.churchofjesuschrist.org/study/ensign/2009/11/more-diligent-and-concerned-at-home

Elder David A. Bednar. "Therefore They Hushed Their Fears" April 2015. https://www.churchofjesuschrist.org/study/general-conference/2015/04/therefore-they-hushed-their-fears?lang=eng

President Ezra Taft Benson (Read by President Thomas S. Monson). "To the Elderly of the Church," Saturday Morning Session, October 1989. https://www.churchofjesuschrist.org/study/general-conference/1989/10/to-the-elderly-in-the-church?lang=eng

About the Author

Michael Callaghan is a software developer with over 25 years of professional experience in the field. Throughout his career, he has developed a reputation as an expert in delivering high-quality software solutions for a wide range of clients and industries. In addition to his technical skills, Michael has found himself speaking in various settings, including giving sacrament talks as a member of The Church of Jesus Christ of Latter-day Saints.

While Michael doesn't consider himself an expert religious speaker, he has experienced the common challenges and pitfalls of public speaking in both spiritual and technical settings. He realized that the skills required for effective communication are universal and applicable to various audiences, including Latter-day Saint congregations.

Michael has written several books on the impact of poor communication on software development projects, which have become widely recognized as essential reading for anyone working in the field. His insights and advice have helped many people avoid costly mistakes and improve the overall quality of their communications.

Follow him on Twitter at https://twitter.com/walkingriver.

Don't miss out!

Visit the website below and you can sign up to receive emails whenever Michael D Callaghan publishes a new book. There's no charge and no obligation.

https://books2read.com/r/B-A-FCXP-VCGUC

BOOKS2READ

Connecting independent readers to independent writers.

Also by Michael D Callaghan

Angular Advocate

Developing Progressive Web Applications with Angular: How to Build and Deploy Mobile Applications without Paying Apple or Google for the Privilege

P-AI-R Programming

P-AI-R Programming: How AI Tools Like GitHub Copilot and ChatGPT Can Radically Transform Your Development Workflow Pair Programming with Chat GPT

Standalone

Don't Say That at Work

Customizing ChatGPT: Quickly and Easily Create and Share Custom Business-Specific GPTs Without Code

How to Deploy Any Web Application to the Apple App Store: Make Your Application Available to Millions of iOS Users in About an Hour with Ionic's Capacitor

Sacrament Talk Mastery: How to Give a Sacrament Talk When You Really Don't Want To

Techno Tales

The Scout Law of Leadership: 12 Attributes Every Leader (or Aspiring Leader) Should Cultivate
¡NO DIGAS ESO EN EL TRABAJO! LECCIONES QUE PUEDES USAR PARA MEJORAR TUS HABILIDADES DE COMUNICACIÓN EN LOS NEGOCIOS

Watch for more at https://walkingriver.com.